THE SCO
COAST TO CC

---

128 MILES WEST TO EAST
FROM OBAN
TO ST. ANDREWS
OVER ROAD, TRACK,
FOREST & FEN

AN
ESSENTIAL GUIDE TO HELP
YOU COMPLETE THE
SCOTTISH COAST TO COAST
WALK

BRIAN SMAILES

BRIAN SMAILES

Holds the record for the fastest 4 and 5 continuous crossings of the Lyke Wake Walk over the North York Moors. He completed the 210 miles over rough terrain on 5 continuous crossings in June 1995 taking 85 hours 50 minutes.

Brian lectures on outdoor pursuit courses and between these travels extensively on walking expeditions and projects.

Long distance running and canoeing are other sports he enjoys, completing 23 marathons and the Caledonian Canal 3 times.

This is Brian's 8th book and most ambitious project to date. It gives me great pleasure to introduce this book as another milestone in his writing career and another challenge completed.

You will never walk alone with these books published by Challenge Publications:-

THE COMPLETE ISLE OF WIGHT COASTAL FOOTPATH
ISBN 0-9526900-6-3

THE YORKSHIRE DALES TOP TEN
ISBN 0-9526900-5-5

JOHN O`GROATS TO LANDS END
ISBN 0-9526900-4-7

THE LAKELAND TOP TEN
ISBN 0-9526900-3-9

THE NATIONAL 3 PEAKS WALK
ISBN 0-9526900-7-1

THE NOVICES GUIDE TO THE YORKSHIRE 3 PEAKS WALK
ISBN 0-9526900-0-4

THE NOVICES GUIDE TO THE LYKE WAKE WALK
ISBN 0-9526900-1-2

ISBN 0-9526900-8-X
First published March 2000
CHALLENGE PUBLICATIONS
7 EARLSMERE DRIVE, BARNSLEY. S71 5HH

ACKNOWLEDGEMENTS

It is with grateful thanks to the following people that this book is published :-

Pam my wife for her support and help on the preparation and subsequent recording of information.

Geoff Whittaker for help in the research of information.

Highlander for clothing supplied and used on the expedition.

ISBN 0-9526900-8-X

Printed by: Dearne Valley Printers Ltd. Tel: 01709 872188

The information recorded in this book is believed by the author to be correct at publication. No liabilities can be accepted for any inaccuracies which may be found. Anyone using this book should refer to the relevant map in conjunction with the book and be experienced in compass use.

The description or representation of a route used does not necessarily mean there is existence of a right of way. Walkers should apply Scottish law, taking into account any local authority information, (see section on Scottish law).

CONTENTS

PLATES

INTRODUCTION

This walk is a test of body, mind and spirit to complete the 128 miles from Oban to St. Andrews. Most of the route is sparsely populated and there are many open aspects over the hillsides and in the glens. Forestry features prominently throughout this walk, having a number of forest sections to complete.

All along the route, the mountain scenery is dramatic and spectacular with deer sightings on the hills and other animal and bird life throughout. Approaching the Perth area the mountains and moorland decrease to be replaced by more fields and farms.

With the wind behind you and the Scottish weather being favourable, you are looking at a minimum of a five day crossing, as I did, but probably around seven days comfortably.

There is not a wide choice of maps available, I used the six maps listed below. Although only 1: 50 000 scale they do give sufficient information to complete this walk.

The relevant maps for this walk are:-

	No's	
O.S. Landranger	49	Oban & East Mull
All 1 : 50 000 scale	50	Glen Orchy
	51	Loch Tay & Glen Dochart
	57	Stirling & The Trossachs
	58	Perth & Alloa
	59	St.Andrews

Oban, your starting point is known as the gateway to the Isles, while St. Andrews is known for the university, cathedral and of course the golf courses.

Between these two towns are a wealth of treasures to see on your journey across Scotland. Plan your expedition carefully to ensure you get maximum pleasure.

Compass bearings have been included where I feel it is necessary, but you will find that for most of the route careful map reading, observation of landmarks and route signs are all that is required. Careful plotting of your route from the grid references provided should ensure you cover the same course as I did.

All compass bearings contained herein are given as magnetic bearings set in 2000.

Below is a table of the magnetic decrease applicable to the maps you will be using

Map		Degrees		Year	Change
49	Mag. North =	4½° w	in	1997	½° in 4 yr.
50 & 57		5° w		1995	1/22° in 4 yr.
58 & 59		5°w		1999	½° in 4 yr.
51		4°w		2000	Ann. change = 13' east

THE LAW RELATING TO FOOTPATHS AND BRIDLEWAYS IN SCOTLAND

Scottish law is quite different to English law in relation to rights of way. User rights by the public is based on custom, therefore maps covering Scotland generally do not show rights of way.

In The Town and Country Planning Act [Scotland] 1972 and in the Countryside [Scotland] Act 1967 :-

A Footpath is a way over which the public have the following but no other rights of way, that is to say a right of way on foot with or without a right of way on pedal cycles.

A Bridleway is a way on which the public have the following but no other rights of way, that is to say a right of way on foot and a right of way on horseback or leading a horse, with or without a right to drive animals of any description along that way.

A Public path is a way which is a footpath or bridleway or a combination of those.

Access to the Countryside under the provisions of The Countryside [Scotland] Act 1967 authorities are empowered to establish rights of access to the countryside. This is not the same as establishing a right of way. It means in simple terms that a person cannot be treated as a trespasser when acting lawfully. Access agreements are not usually applied to "excepted land" which includes agricultural land.

A path shown or described in this book is no indication of a right of way. You need to check your map before you venture on the walk.

It is often said that there is no law of trespass in Scotland, there is, but trespass is not a criminal offence providing you do not cause any damage.

Generally if you are walking sensibly, following the country code and not walking across someone's front garden then you should have no problem. You can still be asked to leave someone's land, and they can use reasonable force to ensure you do leave. In saying this, as long as you do not climb stone walls, damage fences and property, or create a disturbance, then you should be able to follow the route described.

Should you need to wild camp, be unobtrusive and ensure you are not causing a problem by being there, otherwise you could be restrained by a court order. This is known in Scottish terms as restrained by interdict! It is difficult to enforce any law of trespass on the sensible walker who goes about their business lawfully.

In saying all the above in legal terms, I hope it has not confused you even more. I completed the coast to coast on the route described without any problems. In reflection, the biggest problem I had was finding suitable paths in some places rather than metalled road or pavement to walk on. When I found paths or tracks, occasionally they were blocked, overgrown or waterlogged so I had to divert for short distances around the problem.

ROUTE ANALYSIS

The walk starts at the bus station in Oban after first touching the water at the steps down to the sea near the taxi stand. Due to the absence of paths or tracks over land in many places there is a percentage of road walking, most of which is on single track road or pavement. There are sections through forest, on dismantled railway line, and on a Roman Road *[plate 10]*. Other sections take you over grass and peat mountain tracks.

Leaving Oban, the first section to Taynuilt is on single track road *[plate 2]*, but there is opportunity to walk on grass at the side of the road in some areas. I recommend you do this as much as possible to help avoid blisters on the feet caused by walking on hard surfaces.

Passing the old smokery next to Inverawe House you then walk along the Pass of Brander, passing the visitor centre and power station at the side of Lochawe. Kilchurn Castle is at the far end of the loch as you turn right to Dalmally then it is on to the old military road through the forest *[plate 4]*.

After a section of road walking again, you arrive at Tyndrum *[plate 5]*, where there is accommodation, T.I.C. and refreshments available.

Leaving Tyndrum you walk on a section of The West Highland Way, mainly through forest, emerging at the railway station in Crianlarich. The next section is on road and a dismantled railway line, if not too overgrown or built on, before turning off south, ascending alongside Ledcharrie Burn. You climb to over 600m crossing grass and heather on the most difficult section before descending to Kirkton Glen then Rob Roys grave at Balquhidder.

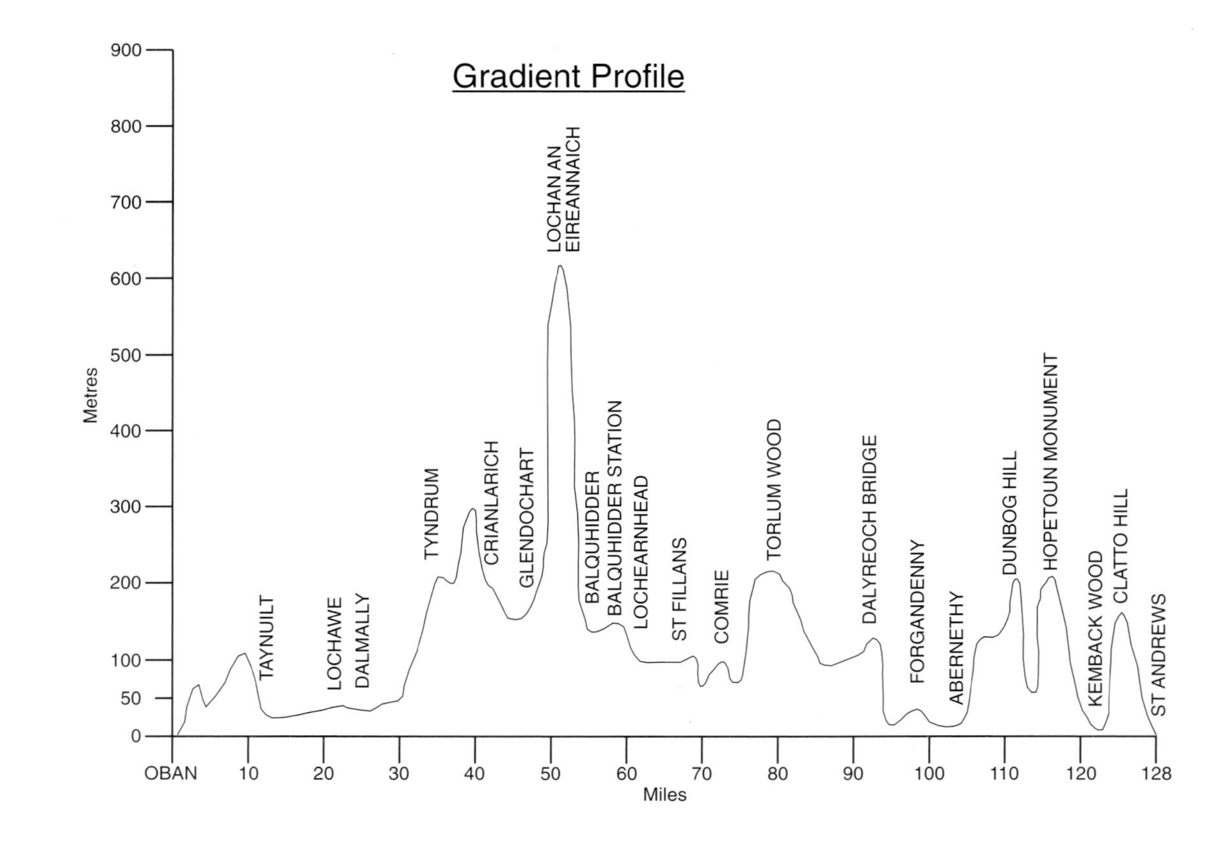

Gradient Profile
Metres
900
800
700
600
500
400
300
200
100
50
0
OBAN
10
20
30
40
50
60
70
80
90
100
110
120
128
Miles
TAYNUILT
LOCHAWE
DALMALLY
TYNDRUM
CRIANLARICH
GLENDOCHART
LOCHAN AN
EIREANNAICH
BALQUHIDDER
BALQUHIDDER STATION
LOCHEARNHEAD
ST FILLANS
COMRIE
TORLUM WOOD
DALYREOCH BRIDGE
FORGANDENNY
ABERNETHY
DUNBOG HILL
HOPETOUN MONUMENT
KEMBACK WOOD
CLATTO HILL
ST ANDREWS

It is by now what seems a long road walk to Lochearnhead *[plate 6]*, then along the side of Loch Earn using the old railway line where possible. Once past St Fillans there is a good stretch of railway path passing a chambered cairn on route.

The scenery has changed now with fewer mountains and more fields, along with villages like Comrie and Abernethy. Passing the entrance to a wildlife centre you walk towards Torlum Wood then Drummond Castle. Soon you are on a Roman Road *[plate 10]* for a few miles, on route to Forgandenny then Abernethy,

With the end nearly in sight you walk towards Lindores Loch then Dunbog Hill where you have a good view of the route ahead to Hopetoun Monument *[plate 11]*.

Passing north of Cupar you walk to Strathkinness where it is downhill all the way to St. Andrews. Walking past the university buildings into the centre you will probably be footsore and weary but there are numerous shops and cafes for refreshment and a well earned rest awaiting you.

This walk is tough and will put your feet to the test, however you will find it helps if you can break it down into shorter sections taking seven or eight days. The absence of regular campsites on route may present a problem but use listed campsites where possible then either wildcamp or stay B&B as I did some nights. Using B&B's enables you to have a bath or shower and probably a good breakfast next morning before starting out. Although you have a planned route, be prepared to re-route slightly if necessary as I had to in some parts.

PREPARATION

It is essential for everyone undertaking this walk to be prepared in terms of physical preparation and familiarisation of the route to be taken.

Physical preparation for this walk means some training which will help you to walk the 128 miles over road, forest track and mountain, probably carrying a heavy rucksack all the way. Some sections are significantly more demanding than others, e.g. from Tyndrum to Balquhidder.

Fitness training should incorporate leg muscle building and stamina training to help you keep a steady pace when walking. Plan a programme of fitness exercises including actual walking up and down hills and get accustomed to carrying a heavy pack.

Physical preparation also means eating the right food to help give your body the energy it needs both before you leave and on the walk itself. Food such as rice, pasta, potatoes, apples and bananas are all good sources of energy when accompanied by protein foods to give you a balanced diet. Try to use dehydrated food where possible to lighten your load and give you more available rucksack space.

It is important to drink regularly and to ensure you carry enough liquid to sustain you on your journey. Unfortunately liquid is heavy to carry but you can make use of cafes etc. on route as I did. An alternative to carrying a lot of liquid is to use water purification tablets added to water from the numerous burns and rivers. The water in the rivers in Scotland generally tends to be very clean, but always use the tablets.

The route to be taken should be studied in detail well before you leave. Using the grid references given, draw your route on the maps with a highlighter pen filling in what in most cases is an obvious route between them.

Check where the campsites/B&B's are on the route and the approximate walking time between. Look in detail at the map to check on the terrain to be covered and build up a picture of your route. Complete a route card with relevant details. Plotting each days journey allows you to plan ahead for the equipment and food required.

EQUIPMENT

Anyone attempting this coast to coast walk should have a reasonable degree of experience in the outdoors as well as knowledge of available equipment and how to use it. Should you be camping or walking unsupported, I feel it is relevant to mention the technical merits and benefits of some of the more important clothing and equipment required for this type of expedition.

Small Tent:- This should be light enough to be carried as a backpacking tent and robust enough to withstand strong winds. A geodesic design will help in this instance. Make sure that the tent is waterproof and not just showerproof. Taped seams will help to both strengthen and keep the tent waterproof.

Sleeping Bag:- This should be light and compact enough to fit into your rucksack - use a compression sack to help it to fit. Should you be purchasing a new sleeping bag, check the material it is made from and whether it is a 4 season bag.

Cooking Stove:- You will need a stove on your expedition unless you are using B&B's and not having hot meals or drinks on route. You may experience strong winds at some time on your journey and in this situation a trangia type of stove is recommended. These are excellent in windy conditions and are quite light and compact to carry. They are fuelled by methylated spirits or gas whichever you prefer.

Overjacket:- This should be water/windproof. There are many types on the market including fleece and other breathable fabrics. Allow space when fitting, for jumpers and other clothing underneath. Deep pockets, a hood and map pocket all help to give full use from this jacket.

Trousers:- Ideally need to be made from cotton or fleece with zipped pockets and a map pocket. The important point is not to wear jeans as they draw the body heat and chafe the skin when wet, they also take a long time to dry.

Gloves/Hat:- These are essential on higher ground or in bad weather as you loose a lot of heat through your head and hands, protect them and stay warm.

Rucksack:- I used a 99 litre rucksack for my 5 day unsupported expedition and although I was careful in selecting equipment, the rucksack was still full *[plate 8]*. Your rucksack should be large enough to hold all your personal and safety equipment. Any rucksack should have wide padded shoulder straps and a waist belt to help prevent movement. Place a large polythene liner inside the bag to keep your clothing dry.

Footwear:- Whichever type of boot you choose they should be comfortable, not too tight, not too slack. They should cover your ankles and have a sewn in tongue. Look after your boots and they will look after you and keep you dry and comfortable. Soft shoes/trainers are useful for the road walking sections or even to give your feet a change of footwear.

Socks/Stockings:- It is important to carry a supply of socks and to change them regularly. Your feet will feel better with a change of socks at least once each day if not more. Changing footwear regularly will also help to prevent blisters by spreading pressure to different parts of the feet.

Personal Clothing:- When you walk from the glen to the peaks or if you stop for a short period of time, you may begin to feel cold very quickly. Carrying extra clothing enables you to put layers on or take layers off to regulate your temperature. A number of thin layers of clothing are better than one thick layer.

Accessories:- Any other equipment you need all takes up space and increases overall weight. Try to use plastic cutlery, cup and plate. Do not take extra large water bottles if a small one will suffice. Similarly you can take de-hydrated food or even stop for some meals. Extra equipment means extra weight and walking 128 miles carrying surplus weight will not help you or your shoulders.

One final word on equipment is to anticipate the conditions you are likely to encounter and take the appropriate clothing but not unnecessary items with you.

ADVICE ON COMPLETING THIS WALK

1. Use a support vehicle to carry any heavy equipment and to supply food on route if available.

2. Eat nourishing and high energy food regularly. Drink liquids frequently.

3. Use good quality clothing and equipment to protect you from the weather, keeping you warm and dry.

4. Footwear should include not only boots but soft shoes/trainers for the road or hard path surfaces to ease pressure on the feet and help prevent blisters. A good supply of walking socks for regular changes also helps.

5. Get an early start each day if possible making full use of daylight hours.

6. Ensure you have a good understanding of map and compass use before you start.

7. Plan and study your route beforehand ensuring you are familiar with places, heights to climb and any foreseeable difficulties that may be encountered.

8. Give a copy of your route and schedule to someone before you leave and maintain daily contact.

9. Try to plan your stops in advance using the campsites or B&Bs described.

10. Take a good supply of blister treatment and treat promptly, do not wait until the blister has appeared before you treat it. Prevention is better than cure. You should also carry a first aid kit.

11. Ensure you do not carry any unnecessary items. It is a long way to carry a heavy rucksack full of unwanted equipment.

12. When on road or hard footpath sections, try to walk on the grass verge as much as possible to ease pressure on the feet.

13. Wear a bright coloured or reflective jacket for the road sections.

14. Follow the country code and be aware of Scottish law relating to access.

15. All compass bearings given herein have been converted to magnetic bearings set in 2000 for your convenience, unless stated.

SAFETY ASPECTS

If you are walking as part of a group it is essential to stay together and for each member of the team to have been involved in planning the route together. Produce a route card and give each team member one as well as leaving a copy with a friend back at base who can monitor your progress.

Only walk the route if it is within the capability of your party. There should be an overall party leader and that person should ensure the group walks at a steady pace, usually the speed of the slowest walker. Observe the country code and use gates and stiles where possible. Above all do not cause damage to property.

Ensure each person carries a survival bag, torch with spare batteries and bulb, whistle and first aid kit as well as spare clothing and some food.

Many people do not realise that a calm sunny day in the glen can mean low cloud and gale force winds on a summit, add this to the wind chill factor and a badly prepared walker has got problems. Bad weather can sweep in quickly. This walk, particularly the sections over higher ground, is not for the inexperienced and should not be attempted without careful planning.

Finally be safe, stay together and be seen, take the correct equipment for the expedition and walk carefully, particularly on the road sections walking on the right in single file, wearing bright clothing if possible.

HYPOTHERMIA

Hypothermia is caused when the body core temperature falls below 35°C. If a walker is not properly prepared for the conditions or the equipment/clothing is not satisfactory then a combination of the cold, wet, exhaustion and the wind chill factor can give a walker hypothermia.

The Signs and Symptoms in Descending Order:-

Shivering
Cold, pale and dry skin
Low body temperature
Irrational behaviour
A gradual slip into unconsciousness
Pulse and respiratory rate slow
Difficulty in detecting breathing and pulse when unconscious
Death

Ways of Preventing Hypothermia

1. Build up body clothing in thin layers, adding on or taking off as necessary.
2. Have suitable wind/waterproofs with you.
3. Take some food/hot drink or boiled sweets which produce energy and heat during digestion.
4. Wear a balaclava/woolly hat to insulate the head, and some gloves.
5. Shelter out of the wind.
6. Take a survival bag and if conditions dictate, use it.

In any type of emergency/accident situation it is always advisable to come off the mountain as soon as possible especially in fog, snow or other bad conditions. The temperature difference between the valley and the summit can be several degrees. If the injured walker is able to move safely, going down the mountain is usually the best solution.

When conditions do not permit movement and if you are in a sheltered area, stay where you are until such time as conditions improve. It may be at this time that you put on extra clothing and use survival bags.

Treatment for Hypothermia

1. Provide extra clothing and shelter from the elements.
2. Bodily warmth of others helps in a gradual warming.
3. If well enough come down into a warmer sheltered area.
4. Give hot drinks if conscious.
5. Give chocolate or sweets if the patient can still take food.
6. The casualty should be placed so that the head is slightly lower than the body.

DO NOT *rub the skin or use a hot water bottle as this can cause a surge of blood from the central body core to the surface, this could prove fatal.*

Alcohol should not be consumed on any walk and should not be given to anyone who has hypothermia. The body temperature will be lowered as well as giving a false sense of security.

THE BODY

RUCKSACK
Containing food, drinks, first aid, clothing, map and compass.
THE HEAD
Should be kept warm, more heat is lost from the head than anywhere else.
THE BODY
Should be kept warm. Build clothes up in layers with wind/waterproofs on top.
HANDS
Should be kept warm with gloves.
MAIN BODY CORE
Temperature must be maintained.
LEGS
It is important not to wear jeans
ANKLES
Should be protected by wearing boots, to help strengthen them.
FEET
Should be kept well cushioned and dry if possible. Good fitting boots will help prevent blisters

THE ROUTE

Start in Oban *[front cover]* near the bus station G.R. 858299 by touching the water at the steps beside the taxi rank. Cross the road from the bus station into Argyll Square *[plate 1]* and walk south east towards the parish church. You pass the Royal Hotel on your left as you leave the town centre. Walk along Combie Street, at the church turn left and ascend to Glen Cruitten Road G.R. 863296. This section leading to Taynuilt is on single track road but you can walk on the grass in a number of places.

Walk along Glen Cruitten Road passing the golf club on your right and some houses on your left. Near the end of the houses a sign to Achavaich points to the left but take the road round to the right following a sign for the rare breeds park.

The road is undulating throughout with some short steep ascents in places. You pass a small tarn or loch on your left. Passing the rare breeds park you come to a junction signposted Connel left and Kilmore right. Turn right here and 600m further on turn left to Taynuilt.

Continue on this undulating road *[plate 2]* crossing over 5 cattle grids and passing a number of farms on the way to Taynuilt. You also pass a standing stone on your left near Strontoiller G.R.909289. Go through a 5 bar gate across the narrow road. Not many vehicles use this road, however you should walk on the grass at the side whenever possible.

You pass the large glasshouses and gardens of Taynuilt Nurseries then the modern holiday chalets called Airdeny Chalets. You arrive in Taynuilt at a junction opposite the war memorial. The Taynuilt Hotel which has B&B is on your left and can be recommended for it's hospitality G.R. 003310.

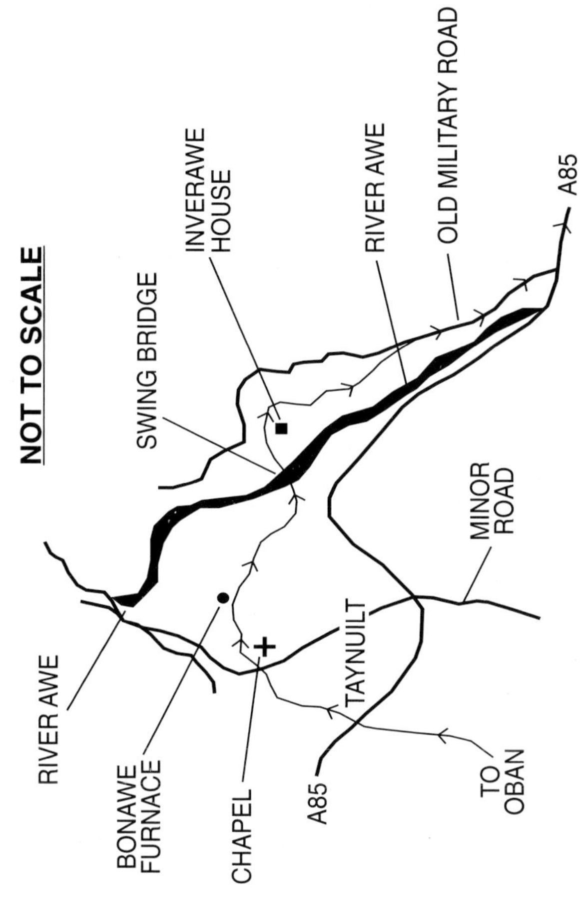

No. 1 TAYNUILT SECTION

To avoid walking on the main road, cross the road onto the B845, walk past the shops, across the bridge over the railway line, descending towards the chapel which you should see ahead. You pass the Allandon B&B on your left. Walk through the housing estate then at a sharp bend in the road turn left going up towards the chapel. You will probably see the small spire.

Just past the chapel turn right up a narrow road leading towards a swing bridge. Walk along the road passing the houses, some with B&B, then passing Bonawe Furnace, a tourist attraction on your left *[plate 3]*. The path turns to a gravel track near a short row of cottages, then forks. You take the right fork walking along a leafy lane, which can be muddy in places. You should see a metal kissing gate on your left G.R. 017314, go through descending to the pedestrian swing bridge spanning the river. Cross, then take the path up to the old smokery and the white building of Inverawe House ahead.

Walk around the side of the smokery, to the front of Inverawe House, a sign states 'No Entry' but this applies only to cars. Follow this metalled road in front of Inverawe House for 2.3km passing another two houses and a small factory unit. This is the old military road leading to the A85.

On reaching the A85 turn left to pass the Crunachy campsite on your right beside a fuel station G.R. 033296. Continue along this busy road leading along the Pass of Brander, walking on the grass where possible. You pass the Awe Barrage as you come to a footpath along the roadside approaching the loch. The power station visitor centre is on your right where refreshments are available.

Continue along the loch side passing the houses at Lochawe village then bearing right around Kilchurn Castle, still on the main A85 road. Passing the entrance to Kilchurn Castle, walk for 3km to Dalmally Hotel. Refreshment is available in the village and hotel. This section is on a long busy road, use any opportunity to walk on the grass at the side, and wear soft shoes on the hard surfaces.

Leave the Dalmally Hotel and walk for 3km passing the B8074 turning at Invelochy on your left. Continue for a further 1.3km on the A85, ascending the hill to a turning left at G.R. 208275 onto the old military road *[plate 4]* leading into the forest, bearing 95°M at the turn off. This is a well defined track just before a slight bend on the main road. Walk on this undulating grass track, which may be wet in places, for 3.3km to meet the A85 road again. Turn left at the road keeping on the grass verge where possible and walk for 4.1km to a left turning onto another section of the old military road. Continue on this again through forest returning to the main road near Arinabea G.R. 294317. Walk again on the road for 3.5km into Tyndrum *[plate 5]* where there are B&B's, camping, bunkhouse, refreshments and inns available and is a good night stop on route.

Leave Tyndrum by walking into the entrance of Pine Trees Leisure Park, G.R. 331300 and descend towards the burn near the forest. Cross the small bridge following the sign for the West Highland Way and turning left through the forest on a well marked path towards Crianlarich. On reaching a cattle grid there is a fork in the path and you need to take the left fork which takes you over a wooden bridge crossing the burn again. The path passes near a white painted house before leading to the side of the River Cononish. Much of the route is waymarked with small yellow arrows.

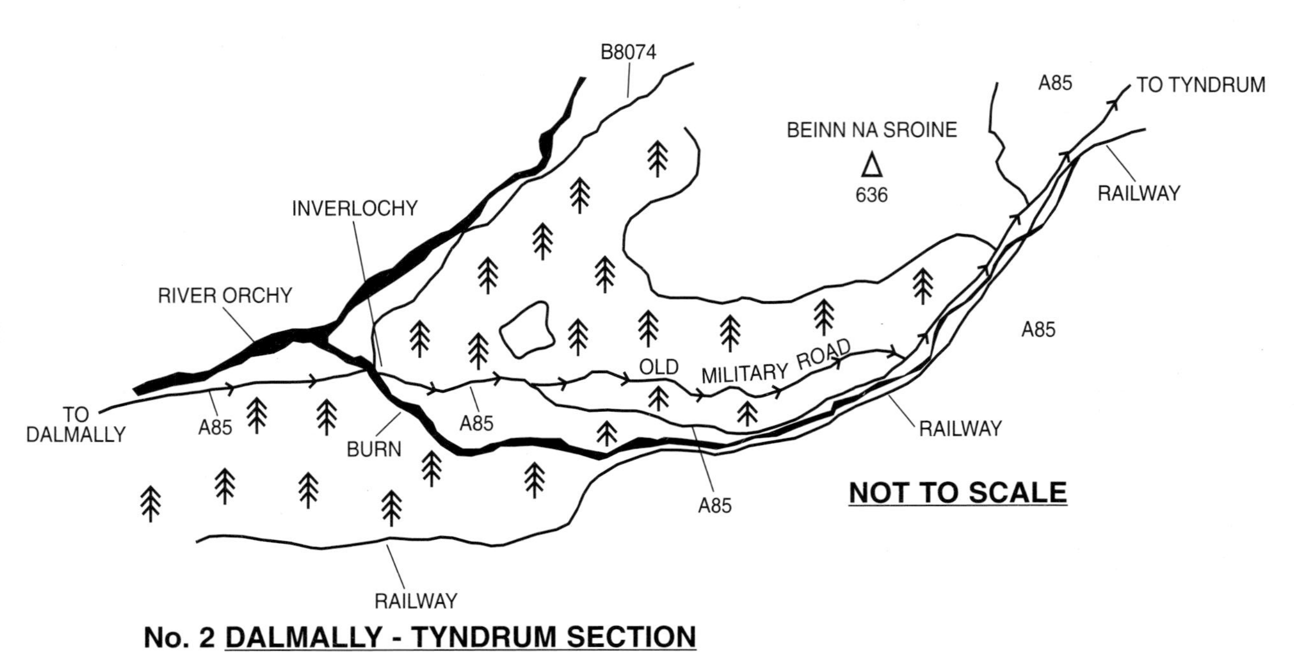

No. 2 DALMALLY - TYNDRUM SECTION

You arrive at a stone bridge with a metalled road over it. Follow the waymark sign crossing the bridge then turn left along the road passing through two 5 bar gates. Strathfillan Parish Church is on your left. At the main road junction further on turn right, walking for 2km before turning right into the forest again back onto the West Highland Way at G.R.363272.

Ascend now for 3.5km on an obvious, stony, undulating path and track which is steep in places, over burns and through the forest towards Crianlarich. You eventually come to a large kissing gate. The West Highland Way turns right here and is signed, but go straight ahead towards Crianlarich. Continue on this forest path for a short distance before descending steeply to Crianlarich, emerging opposite the railway station.

Cross the main A82 road and go through the subway to the village centre passing a youth hostel on the way. At the junction beside Crianlarich village hall, turn right, walking on the grass beside the A85 road and passing the Ben More Lodge hotel on your left. The disused railway track is on your left also. A cottage just past the hotel has a five bar gate at the side which should take you onto the track.

Walk along the old railway track, or if overgrown or blocked, which you may find in parts, depending on the time of year, walk on the grass at the side of the main road. You come to a five bar gate on the railway track and a wider gravel track ahead on the same route. You should see some white painted houses on your right with Ben More towering alone behind. You go through a small metal gate between the houses to the main road. Turn left walking for 7km to the sign for Glen Dochart camping and caravan park, G.R. 477279.

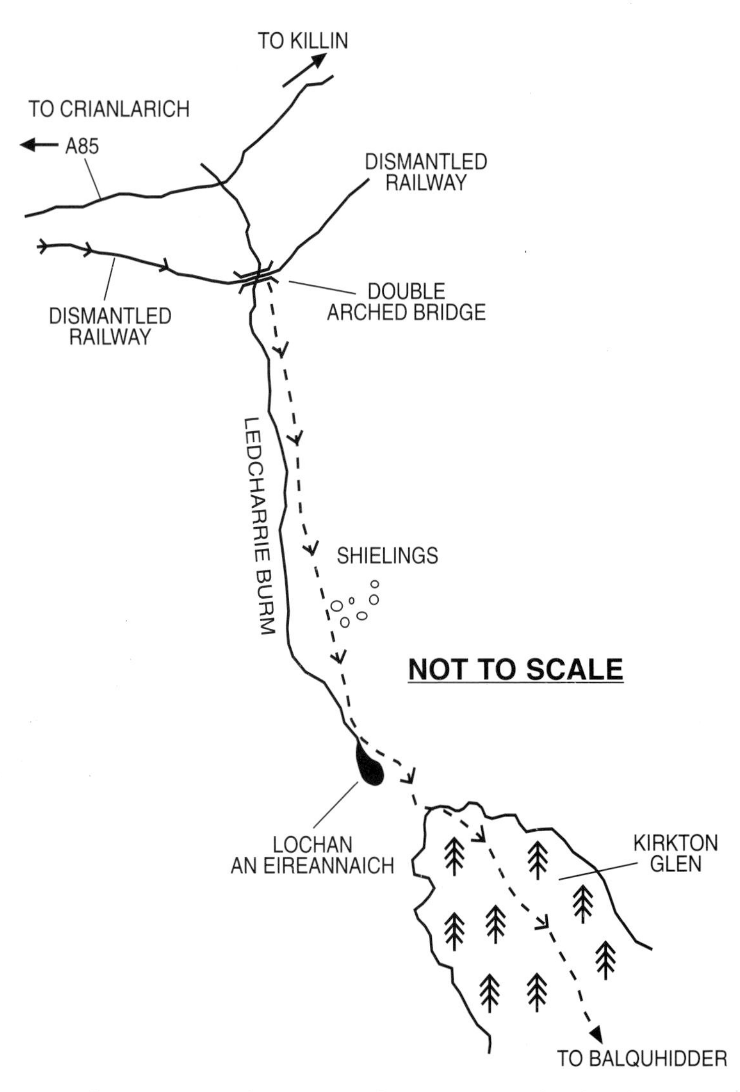

No. 3 CRIANLARICH - BALQUHIDDER SECTION

The disused railway line can be picked up again at the caravan park. This may be a convenient place to stay overnight. The next section to Balquhidder is the toughest of your journey so you should start if possible refreshed after a nights rest.

You are on the right side of the main road at the caravan park where you pick up the railway line again. Continue on it for 3.1km to a double arched bridge over a burn. Ensure you find the correct bridge which crosses Ledcharrie Burn. You pick up a feint path bearing 200°M off to your right and ascending steeply for 4.6km to Lochan an Eireannaich at G.R. 515244 to the right of the summit. At the loch follow the path for a short distance bearing 124°M from the north end of the loch towards the forest then on a track descending through Kirkton Glen to Balquhidder. You emerge near the church and Rob Roys grave at G.R. 536210

Turn left at the church in Balquhidder walking on the minor road for 2.9km to the A84 road. Turn left beside the hotel walking along the roadside to Balquhidder station where there is a campsite available. Continue on this road for 3.6km to the road junction with the A85 in Lochearnhead *[plate 6]*.

In Lochearnhead turn right then left along the side of the village hall walking along Auchraw Terrace. Turn left passing Lochearn Lodges on a wide gravel track, a wood chalet is on your right. You go onto the disused railway track at the side of the small bridge but it may be overgrown depending on the time of year, in which case you should access it through the nearby field.

Plate 1
Argyll Square, Oban. The beginning of your journey.

Plate 2

Just past the rare breeds park between Oban and Taynuilt at G.R. 892292

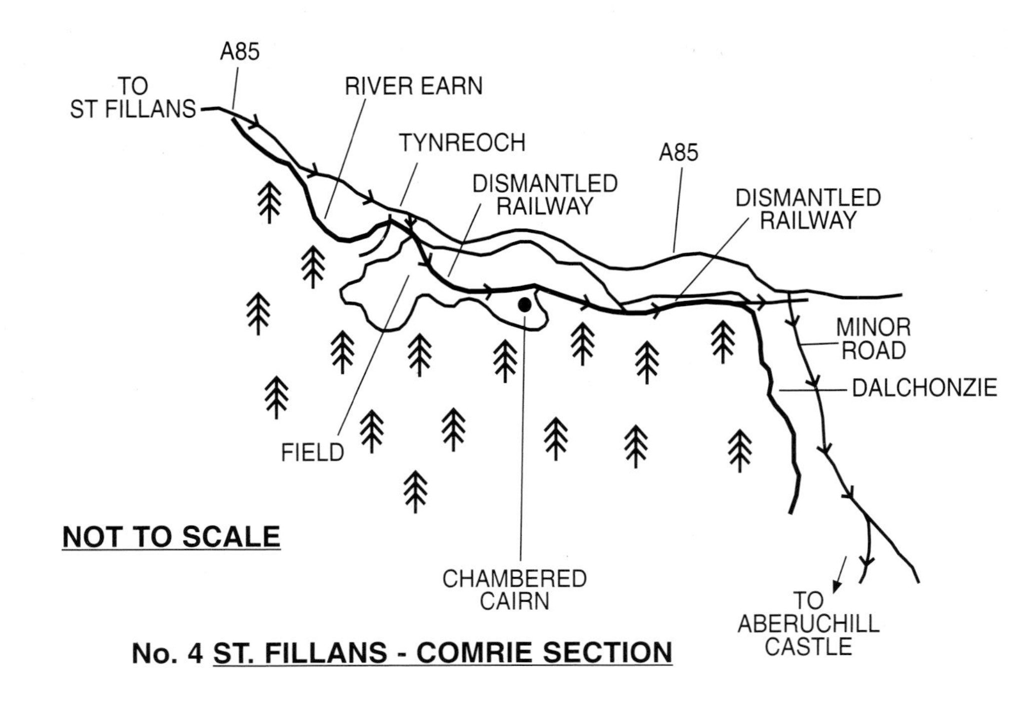

No. 4 ST. FILLANS - COMRIE SECTION

On the railway track there are good views of Loch Earn. Ideally you should try to stay on this track, passing St. Fillans, until you get to Tynreoch but you may find as I did that parts are blocked or waterlogged, in this situation descend to the road walking along the lochside to Tynreoch. The railway track improves further along just past St. Fillans, so look for paths leading back to the track to avoid walking on the road.

Leave the railway track at Tynreoch, walk a short distance on the road to a narrow minor road off to your right. You should see two stone pillars at the roadside with Dundurn written on them at G.R. 714235. Go between the two pillars following the road around to your left and going over a metal bridge spanning the river. Cross the bridge and you should see a 5 bar gate on your left and another leading straight on with a track off to your right. Take the middle track through the gate marked private bearing 149°M from the gate. This takes you onto a good stretch of railway track for 3km to Dalchonzie. You pass an interesting chambered cairn on your right which is worth a close inspection. It is a pleasant walk on this section.

You go through a 5 bar gate onto the minor road where you turn right towards the small power station 1km down the long straight road. Cross a stone bridge over the River Earn which leads to the power station beside East Dundurn Wood. You see a 5 bar gate 450m past the power station at G.R. 745217. Take this path through the gate passing two large trees just inside.

Follow the path through the field where it soon bears right, leading round to Aberuchill Castle *[plate 7]*. Crossing the field you see some

Plate 3
Bonawe Furnace near Taynuilt. G.R. 011318

Plate 4

The turning onto the Old Military Road between Dalmally and Tyndrum at G.R. 208275

white gates at the left of the castle at G.R. 746212. Go through then turn left onto the access road taking you over a small bridge then passing some buildings on your right. Just past the buildings a track bears off right which you take towards Craggish. Continue, going over two cattle grids and passing four houses, on this stony track which is south of Ross Wood *[plate 9]*.

On reaching the minor road at Craggish continue straight ahead for 1km passing Earthquake House which is just off the road on your left. Cross the stone humpback bridge then turn right to pass the church with spire, into Comrie. This is a good place to get refreshment and replenish food stocks. In the village centre, cross the impressive stone bridge spanning the River Earn. Go down the long straight B827 road through Dalginross. At the end of the road go straight across onto Cowden Road. Continue to the far end of the houses going towards Cowden, picking up a wide gravel track leading towards the fields.

You come to a narrow metalled road going through a white 5 bar gate. A sign states Cowden House, where you walk down the driveway. Just before the first cottage on the bend G.R. 780206, turn right over a stile then along by the barbwire fence to the trees at the end of the field. Cross a small stile then ascend the hill, bearing 158°M from the stile. While ascending the hill look for the 5 bar gate which you go through to the top of the hill.

Descend keeping the small loch you can see ahead off to your left. Go through a 5 bar gate beside a kissing gate, and walk along a grass track leading to the road at G.R. 780197. Go through another kissing gate to emerge onto the minor road. Turn right then immediately left onto the B827 following the signs to the wildlife centre.

Walk up the hill and past the wildlife centre offices towards Auchingarrich, then onto a forest track at the far end of the buildings. Take a bearing of 180°M at the beginning of the track then ascend through the forest for 1km. Turn off just after a sharp left hand bend bearing 154°M to take you near a strip of woodland. Cross over several fields to the minor road just south east of Craigneich Farm at G.R.804174.

Walk along this minor road passing an old farm called Craggan, then 300m after it turn off through a tall gate on a track to Torlum Wood following the obvious track up to the forest. The path ascends steeply then skirts around the south side of the wood. Once on the high ground after rounding the bend, go over some steps spanning the deer fence onto a distinctive forest track at G.R. 818178, leading gradually down to the sawmill. Keep referring to your map but generally stay on the south side of the forest which is the main path to the sawmill.

At the Drummond estates sawmill turn right out of the entrance onto the road walking for 300m down into a dip in the road, turning left opposite the second house on your right. Walk along this track bearing 106°M from the road entrance, following an obvious track towards Muthill.

Arriving at a farm cottage in the field, go through a 5 bar gate at the side then take a bearing of 93°M turning left to cross the fields towards Muthill. Use the gates for access into each field.

Keep walking in this straight line, referring to your map, to join a track leading to the main A822 road at G.R. 855176. This land is owned by Drummond estates and you should not deviate from your route. You will see the town of Crieff off to your left in the distance just before you reach Muthill. Keep on the higher ground to your right well away from Drummond Castle area.

Plate 5
Entering Tyndrum at G.R. 327307

Plate 6

Passing through Lochearnhead, your route is off to the right along Loch Earn. G.R. 589238

Arriving at the A822 road go through the double 5 bar gate then cross the road following a track between the houses to Fintalich farm at the far end. Bear right at the farm taking you through two 5 bar gates into a field. Bearing 175°M from the gates, follow the distinctive track towards a small wood. Walk alongside it before passing some houses and emerging onto a minor road 500m from Muthill village centre.

Turn left on the narrow metalled road walking for 3.4km to Innerpeffray passing Strageath Mains. Cross the River Earn just before the chapel. Ensure you do not turn onto any of the other minor roads, left or right, on the way to Innerpeffray. Your route from Innerpeffray is now along the old Roman Road for 8km before turning off towards Gask House. This track is more evident in some places than others. The route crosses minor roads six times in the first 2km and you must also walk around two buildings. At the chapel at Innerpeffray take a bearing of 88°M and pick up the Roman Road leading to Parkneuk Cottage. Stay on this bearing for 1.4km from the cottage until you reach the minor road to the east of Shearston farm. You may need to walk around the side of some fields along this section, but ensure you reach G.R. 929187.

Cross the minor road then take bearing 90°M to a small wood. Walk along the wooded side of the fence crossing a stile into a field, leading into the main wood. Continue through the wood which may be overgrown in places, with no visible path although it is marked on the map. Should it prove too difficult to go through the wood, refer to the map then navigate around it as it is only small. I managed to get through but did find it difficult in some places. You should pick up the Roman Road again on the far side at G.R. 939188 *[plate 10]*.

You go through several 5 bar gates then past a Roman signal station on this straight track. Arriving at another forest keep to the left side of it still following the previous bearing. Pass another signal station as you walk on the grass track at the side of the forest where an information plaque is displayed. On the final section of the Roman Road before you turn off, there are impressive views of the mountains in the far distance left and right.

You come to a 5 bar gate leading onto a minor road which you walk along, still following the same bearing. A forest is in front and a sign states private woods, but it is open for walkers. Continue on a long straight gravel track through the wood, then when the forest track bears off to the right, you carry straight on, bearing 91°M from the bend in the track, while referring to your map.

Walk through the trees, then along the side of a field with the forest on your right, still staying on a feint track. Keep near the side of the field to a ruined farm called Muir o'Fauld [you may need to climb over two old disused wooden gates], where you join a good distinctive track taking you to a minor road 900m further on.

When you come to a 5 bar gate at the minor road, turn right walking for 150m on a metalled road. There are two gates near the bend, one straight ahead and one to the left. Take the left one, initial bearing 82°M at the road, refer to your map and follow the track clockwise through the wood. It can be wet and overgrown in places. Go through a tall gate in the deer fence, staying on the track leading towards Gask House. The rough track ends as you leave the forest and you come onto a straight farm track for 700m at G.R. 990188 bringing you behind the large impressive building of Gask House.

Plate 7
Passing Aberuchill Castle beside east Dundurn Wood on route to Comrie. G.R. 746212

Plate 8
Tent pitched for the night and time to relax.

Walking around to the far side of Gask House, take the second driveway on the left looking down towards Dalreoch Bridge and the River Earn. Descend this long metalled narrow driveway, where you can walk on the grass at the side, to the minor road 1.1km further on. Turn right at the junction walking for 300m down the lane to another lane on your left at G.R. 005181.

Continue on this lane for 1.4km before descending to the A9 dual carriageway opposite the third small strip of woodland on the south side of the A9 at G.R.019179. Cross the dual carriageway with extreme care then join a track just below the main road leading north east, initially ascending steeply then undulating to Wester Cairnie farm.

Continue to the B934 road 500m further on then turn right descending a hill to the bridge over the River Earn which you should now see 1km in front. Turn right going over the bridge onto a long straight road walking for 900m then turn left onto the B935 to Forgandenny 4.1km further on. Walk through the village still on the B935 to Eastfield at G.R. 094180. As the road bears left on a slight bend leaving the village, you bear right on a stony track which becomes a narrow metalled road, leading towards South Dumbuils. Continue up the lane towards the brow of the hill, turn left at a fork in the track bearing 77°M at the fork and crossing several fields to Mount Stewart. Walk around the field perimeters if they are planted, using gates for entry.

Reaching Mount Stewart farm, either cross the fields to a service track leading to Pitkealthy Wells farm, bearing 96°M from Mount Stewart, or continue down the farm track to the main road at Baxterknowe. Turn right there taking care on the busy road as you walk for 1km to the entrance to Pitkealthy Wells farm.

Just along the lane you see a sign for Silver Walk. Turn here through the kissing gate at G.R. 116177 on a pleasant walk for 800m to another kissing gate at a road. Turn left at the metalled road and walk for 1.3km into Bridge of Earn.

Follow the minor road turning right to Kintillo when you see the sign opposite Kilgraston school. Walk through the housing estate, turning left at a junction then right along Old Edinburgh Road. You go under the railway bridge [refer to map], then turn right under the M90 motorway on Clayton Road. Pass the old hospital on your left and follow the signs towards Elliothead and Culfargie. You will see Abernethy just off to your right 5km further on.

You come to a very long straight metalled road between the open fields leading to Kulfargie. Follow this road eventually rounding a bend, passing the farm then arriving at a small concrete bridge. Cross the bridge following the track around to your right and walking anti-clockwise towards the railway line. You come to a single house at Carey. Keep left at a small gas tank as you approach Carey then the track winds it's way towards the railway line again. You pass under the railway arch walking up a metalled road before turning left through Abernethy centre.

Walk along the main street passing the Abernethy Hotel on your right which has B&B as well as bar meals. Leaving the hotel, continue along the main street for 1.5km, turning right between the electricity pylons and the railway bridge. Ascend towards Pitcairlie Hill passing West Greenside Farm. Looking back there are good views of the River Tay.

Plate 9
Walking through Ross Wood just after Aberuchill Castle at G.R. 753209

Plate 10
The section of Roman Road 3.6 kms east of Innerpeffray at G.R. 938188

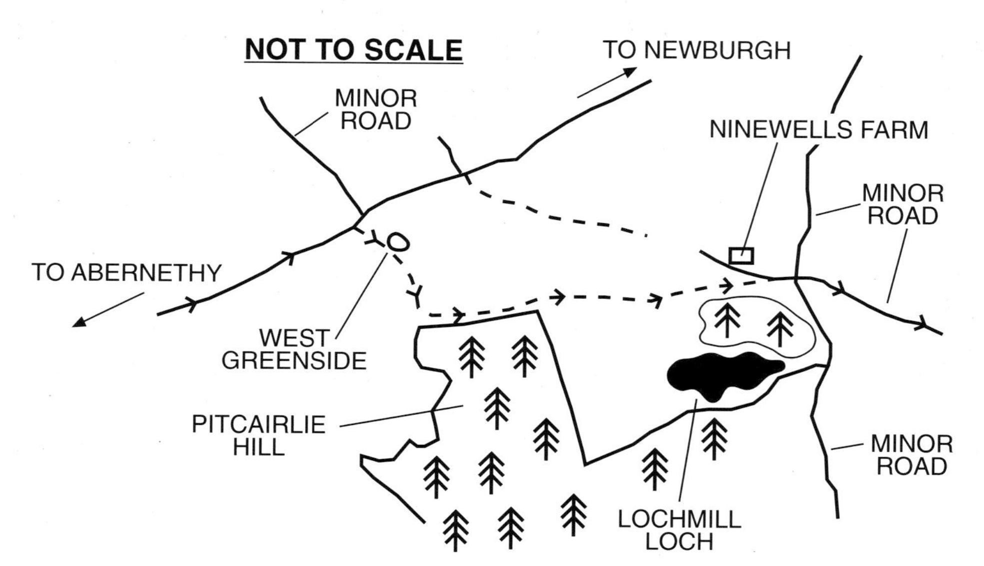

No. 5 ABERNETHY - LINDORES SECTION

Ascend the hill on a track towards the corner of the forest G.R. 205165. Bear left towards Ninewells farm, leaving the forest to your right and passing below some crags, also on your right. Walk towards the left side of the next wood as you go towards the minor road junction just east of Ninewells farm. Arriving at the junction, go across towards Whinnybank, then pass Thane Croft on your left followed by several blocks of cottages and a few houses on both sides of the road.

On a sharp bend is a clump of trees with a short distinctive track at the side of it. Follow this into the field and walk around the field to the far corner. Cross the road, turn left, walk for a short distance before turning right to take you up a track near Halton Hill at G.R. 243163. At the top of this track it bears left descending to Grange of Lindores.

Walk through the village where you see Lindores Loch slightly off to your right. Your route goes clockwise around the loch. In the village you walk along a street called The Paddocks, turning left then immediately right to go down by the small parish church marked on the map at G.R. 257167. Cross over the railway bridge next to the church following the road to Lindores. At the main A913 road junction turn right walking for 250m to the B937 bearing off right.

With Lindores Loch on your right, walk along this road for 1.2km to the gatehouse to Inchrye, here you turn left at G.R. 273162 on a track to the summit of Dunbog Hill. The track ascends steeply then bears off right halfway up to take you along the side of a small plantation, then through a small wooden gate. Another plantation is higher up as the track still ascends steeply between Whitefield and Dunbog Hill before levelling and winding round to Dunbog Hill on the far side at G.R. 287164.

Plate 11
Looking towards Hopetoun Monument from just east of Collairniehill at G.R. 300164

Plate 12
Ascending through Kemback Wood at G.R. 428158

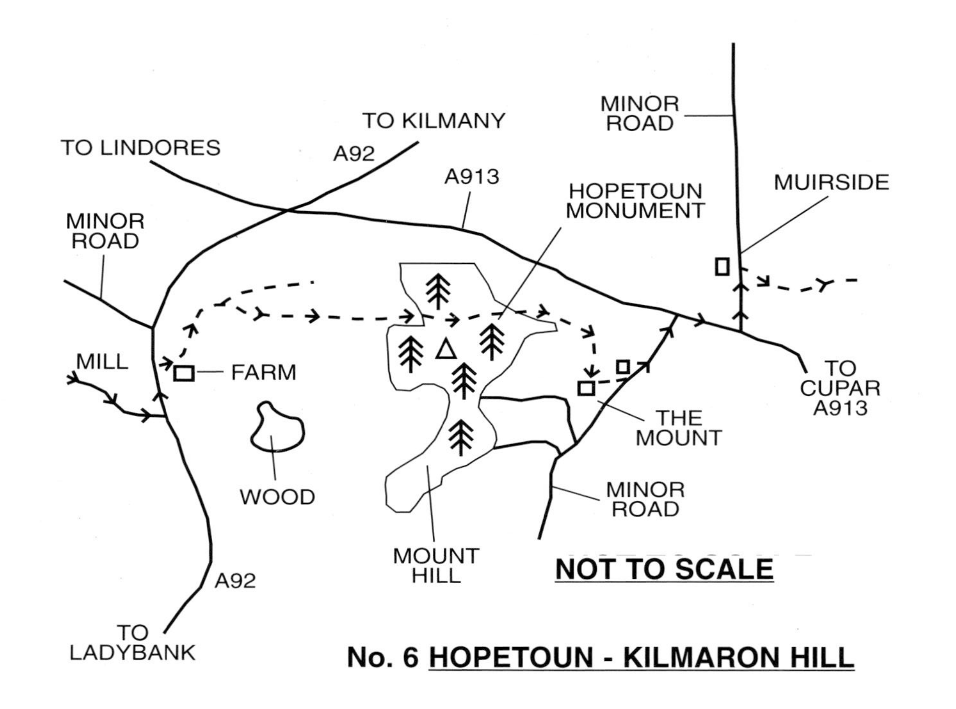

No. 6 HOPETOUN - KILMARON HILL

On the summit of Dunbog Hill you can see your route in the far distance stretching across to Hopetoun Monument on a hill at G.R. 331165. Take time here to observe the land layout and take your bearings, plotting your route to the left side of the forest on Mount Hill, bearing 92°M from Dunbog Hill. I plotted as near a straight line as possible walking around fields and woodland where necessary towards the left side of Hopetoun Monument *[plate 11]* on Mount Hill.

Descend Dunbog Hill, then cross several fields on a pleasant walk over undulating countryside before descending to a farm track at G.R. 304165. This track takes you along the right side of some woodland *[plate 11]* and leads down to Cunnoquhie Mill. You may see your path ascending the left side of Mount Hill ahead. Follow the track descending gradually to the main A92 road.

Joining the A92 take care on this busy road and turn left, walking for 350m to the entrance to Lindifferon, which is a farm with outlying cottages. Turn right ascending past the farm on your right to a 5 bar gate at the side of the row of cottages. Go through this and another 5 bar gate to ascend a steep track which winds it's way to the summit. You come to a large water tank, continue to ascend straight up the hillside to two 5 bar gates, go through, and walk to the far corner of the forest at G.R. 331167 where there is a gate leading into the forest.

Walk through the gate, initially bearing right then left on a path to the far side. You do not go to the monument itself. Once at the far side orientate your map and check your bearing and route from this vantage point. You should see Cupar to your right approx. bearing 124°M with St. Andrews in the far distance ahead. As you descend, the track winds around a strip of woodland to a farm called The Mount. Walk around the farm buildings to some bungalows, 300m further along the pebbled driveway, to a minor road before turning left and walking for 500m to the main road.

Turn right at the main A913 road, again walking for 500m to a sign to Moonzie, Luthrie and Rathillet where you turn left to Muirside cottage 500m further up. Your route is opposite Muirside bearing 112°M from the cottage, on a distinctive farm track going east towards Cairnie Lodge. You see two clumps of trees on your right and your path goes between them.

Walk on the obvious track in a straight line towards the lodges. Initially the track is narrow as you ascend, then it widens giving easy walking on grass along Kilmaron Hill, where you can set a brisk pace.

Arriving at the main road near Hilton House, turn right walking for 250m to a minor track on your left leading to Foodieash 800m further on. A telephone kiosk is at the side of the small village green with a cluster of houses around it. Cross the minor road in Foodieash to pick up a path which ascends across a field, [this may be ploughed], at G.R. 381165. Cross the field ascending to the trees you see directly ahead on bearing 110°M from the base of the field.

You will find the track at the top blocked with rubble for some distance, so walk along the side of the field until you can find a way onto the track. This track leads to a minor metalled road and the A91 is 1km ahead. Cross the A91 onto a stony farm track with some grass in the centre to walk on. Stay on this good track right to a castle and church at G.R. 414162 which you should see in front. The track forks at one point but keep left towards the castle and church.

Just before the minor road at Dairsie Mains you pass a row of cottages before coming to a farm. Turn right at the farm to take you over the railway to the castle, then to the church. Descend the hill passing the church then cross the impressive stone bridge over the river. A sign near the bridge states St. Andrews 6 miles, by road.

Walk over the bridge and go around the left side of the large forest in front of you, still on the road. The River Eden is on your left as you walk along the metalled road to Kinnaird Farm. Passing the farm, you walk for 500m to two cottages at G.R. 426164 where you bear right along the side of the cottages into the wood.

Walk for a short distance along the lower edge of the wood before ascending on a steep path through Kemback Wood. The route twists and turns and ascends steeply through thick forest on a distinctive path to the top at G.R. 428156. You emerge beside some houses on a narrow metalled road, walk a few metres to a kissing gate then descend over a field to another kissing gate.

Turn left on a narrow pebbled road passing some houses. This road becomes a narrow metalled road. Turn left at a junction, towards Strathkinness. The road ascends for a short distance as you pass a telephone box on your left at G.R. 430153. Walk past all the houses then the road turns to a gravel track.

Just over the brow of Clatto Hill you have a good view of St. Andrews in the distance. Follow the distinctive track descending slightly to a farm which you walk past. Continue to a fork in the track [refer to your map closely at this point] then take the left fork along a strip of grass to Bonfield at G.R. 451161.

Proceed along this path at the side of the field onto a narrow road between some houses called Bonfield Road and continue into Strathkinness. At the cross-roads you will see the church ahead of you. Cross the road in the village, walking along Church Road to pass the church and the playing fields near the end of the road. There are good views of the sea and St. Andrews from here.

Turn right at the junction for the final approach to St. Andrews on the 'B' road. There are fields on your left and houses on your right as you proceed. The pavement stops at the end of the houses so you should walk with care on the road for a short distance into St. Andrews. You may see the castle ruins and a number of church towers as you look across to the town.

You pass Whitecroft guest lodges as you enter the town. The route is flat into the centre as you walk through the housing estate passing some university buildings on the way. Follow the signs to the town centre and shopping area. Walk down the main street past the shops to the tourist information centre on the right, cross the road following the signs to the castle on the cliff beside the sea *[front cover].*

Beside the castle there is a ramp to walk down to the sea where you can touch the water. Your expedition is over! Going back into the town centre, the bus station is at the opposite end of the main high street near the roundabout.

PLACES OF INTEREST ON ROUTE

Oban has been in existence for about 200 years and is a busy gateway to the numerous islands which lie off the coastline. In Oban there is a whisky distillery and McCaig's Tower *[front cover],* a folly built in 1897 to provide employment. There are museums, Caithness glassworks and castles, in particular Gylan Castle on Kerrera island near Oban which was once the stronghold of the Mac Dougall clan.

Bonawe near Taynuilt famous for the Bonawe Furnace which has been restored along with the cottages and casting house as it was in the 18th century.

Kilchurn Castle [Dalmally] dating from the 15th century and the Campbell stronghold, is impressive at the side of Loch Awe.

Tyndrum It's claim to fame was that Robert the Bruce lost a brooch near Tyndrum. The village is a staging post on journeys to northern Scotland being a central point on the main trunk road north.

Balquhidder holds the grave of Rob Roy, the legendary Scottish rebel who died in 1740 and is buried in the local churchyard.

Lochearnhead is a centre for waterskiing and yachting on the loch of the same name.

St. Fillans is overlooked by Dunfillan Hill 2011ft. which has a rock on top known as St.Fillans chair, once a fortified site used by the Picts.

Comrie is an area famed for earth tremors, the first recorded in 1872. Earthquake House is nearby and the village brews earthquake ale, sold in the Royal Hotel.

Drummond Castle was originally built in 1491 and has extensive gardens.

Forgandenny is overlooked by Culteuchar Hill at 1028ft. which has remains of an old fort.

Abernethy has one of only two round towers in Scotland on it's parish church dating from the 12th century. The town was once the capital of the picts.

St. Andrews is famous for many things including the golf courses and tournaments, the cathedral, originally dating back to 1160 and St. Andrews Castle *[front cover]*, on the cliffs above the north sea. St. Rule's church has a famous square tower and 158 steps to the top. Good views of the town in all directions can be had from the top and it is worth the effort getting there, even after completing 128 miles.

Grid References on Route

Oban	G.R.859299	Torlum Wood	G.R.830179
Glen Cruitten	G.R.866296	Drummond Trk.	G.R. 839176
Glen Cruitten	G.R.878299	Farm Track	G.R. 852175
Rare Breeds Park	G.R.890292	Fintalich	G.R. 870178
Near Cairn	G.R.916286	Crossroads	G.R. 892182
Airdenny	G.R.992292	Roman Road	G.R. 929187
Brochroy	G.R.005315	Muir o' Fauld	G.R. 978190
Bonawe Furnace	G.R.016315	Gask House	G.R. 996189
Inverawe House	G.R.022316	Farm Track	G.R. 021179
Military Road	G.R.032302	Minor Road	G.R. 045182
Visitor Centre	G.R.073270	Eastfld. Trn. Off	G.R.094180
Drishaig	G.R.132284	Mount Stewart	G.R.106174
Dalmally	G.R.163273	Silver Walk	G.R.116177
Old Military Rd.	G.R.208275	Minor Road	G.R.128171
A85 Road	G.R.244284	Minor Road	G.R.139179
Tyndrum	G.R.330303	Culfargie	G.R.168177
West H/land Way	G.R.337290	Carey	G.R.175169
A82 W.H.W. Turn	G.R.360276	Abernethy A913	G.R.195167
Crianlarich	G.R.388253	Sth. Of Bloomfld.	G.R.217167
Portnellan	G.R.410258	Minor Road	G.R.227168
Cm/ping & Turning	G.R.474280	Minor Road	G.R.247159
Ledcharrie Burn	G.R.508270	To Dunbog Hill	G.R.272162
Kirkton Glen[Forest]	G.R.530226	Dunbog Hill	G.R.288164
Auchtubh	G.R.560207	Cunnoquie Mill	G.R.310163
Lochearnhead	G.R.589238	Mount Hill Path	G.R.331167
Dalveich	G.R.617245	Access Road	G.R.342163
Tynreoch	G.R.714235	Muirside	G.R.350170
Railway Track	G.R.727230	Track	G.R.371165
East Dundurn Wood	G.R.745217	Minor Road	G.R.398160
Ross Wood	G.R.751210	Bridge	G.R.416161
Comrie	G.R.773220	Kemback Wood	G.R.427160
Cowden	G.R.780206	Minor Road	G.R.433155
Wildlife Centre	G.R.789194	Church	G.R.460163
Minor Road	G.R.802175	Minor Road	G.R.483165
Craggan Tn Off	G.R.817169	St. Andrews	G.R.514168

Campsites

Oban
caravan & camping park 01631 562425
Gallanach Road,
Oban.
[1.5 miles from town centre]

Taynuilt
Crunachy caravan & camping park 01866 822612
Bridge of Awe
Taynuilt

Tyndrum
Pine Trees leisure park 01838 400243
Tyndrum
[caravan, camping & bunkhouse, recommended].

Crianlarich
Glendochart caravan & camping park 01567 820637
Glendochart

Lochearnhead
Balquhidder Braes car. & camping pk. 01567 830293
Balquhidder Station
Lochearnhead

St. Andrews
Cairnsmill caravan & camping park 01334 473604
Largo Road
St. Andrews
[Situated on outskirts of town]

Unless stated, all sites are on your route.

B & B's on Route

Oban	Mrs Barr	01631 566392
	Mrs Worthington	01631 564601
	Mrs Aires	01631 562260
	Mrs Barnett	01631 565413
	Harbour View Guest Hse.	01631 563462
Taynuilt	Taynuilt Hotel	01866 822437
	Mrs Gillies	01866 822351
Dalmally	Mrs Mac Dougall	01838 200373
	Mrs Borrett	01838 200496
Tyndrum	Glengarry Guest House	01838 400224
Crianlarich	Craigbank Guest Hse.	01838 300279
	Mrs Anderson	01838 300253
	Dunfraoich	01838 300277
Balquhidder	Mr Campbell	01877 384635
Lochearnhead	Orchard Lodge	01567 830317
Abernethy	Abernethy Hotel	01738 850220
Cupar	Mrs Stewart	01334 652798
	One mile off route.	
	Mr Duncan	01334 652569
	One mile off route.	
St Andrews	Mrs Rhind	01334 475677
	Mrs Sheridan	01334 473408
	Mrs Methven	01334 474574
	Mrs Mair	01334 472709

Approximate Walking Times
Between Prominent Landmarks

		Hrs.	Min.
Oban	- Taynuilt	4	30
Taynuilt	- Dalmally	5	00
Dalmally	- Tyndrum	5	00
Tyndrum	- Crianlarich	3	15
Crianlarich	- Glendochart Campsite	2	30
Glendochart	- Balquhidder	5	10
Balquhidder	- Lochearnhead	1	45
Lochearnhead	- St Fillans	2	50
St Fillans	- Comrie	2	10
Comrie	- Torlum Wood [Sawmill]	3	20
Sawmill	- Dalreoch Bridge	4	50
Dalreoch Bridge	- Forgandenny	2	30
Forgandenny	- Abernethy	3	00
Abernethy	- Dunbog Hill	3	15
Dunbog Hill	- Hopetoun Monument	2	00
Monument	- Kemback Wood Entrance	2	30
Kemback Wood	- St Andrews Castle	2	50

Walking the complete route will take a minimum of five days but expect to take around seven days for this 128 mile route. Walking times will vary considerably depending on size and fitness of the group, weather conditions, weight of pack carried and amount of climbing required. Completing this walk can be a stiff task for anyone while carrying full equipment, especially in bad weather conditions.

Distances Between Prominent Landmarks
Calculated to include ascents and descents.

		Km	Miles
Oban	- Taynuilt	18.7	11.62
Taynuilt	- Dalmally	20.1	12.5
Dalmally	- Tyndrum	19.2	11.93
Tyndrum	- Crianlarich	8.44	5.24
Crianlarich	- Glendochart C.site	10.0	6.21
Glendochart Campsite	- Balquhidder	11.2	7.0
Balquhidder	- Lochearnhead	7.4	4.6
Lochearnhead	- St Fillans	11.5	7.2
St Fillans	- Comrie	9.3	5.8
Comrie	- Torlum Wood S'mill	10.6	6.6
Sawmill	- Dalreoch Bridge	18.9	11.7
Dalreoch Bridge	- Forgandenny	10.3	6.4
Forgandenny	- Abernethy	12.3	7.64
Abernethy	- Dunbog Hill	11.35	7.05
Dunbog Hill	- Hopetoun Monument	5.52	3.43
Hopetoun Monument	- Kemback Wood Ent.	11.16	6.93
Kemback Wood Ent.	- St Andrews Castle	10.08	6.26
		206.05	128.11

The Scottish Coast to Coast Walk involves walking 128 miles on road, track, path and over mountains. A good degree of fitness, map recognition and navigational skills are required, along with general experience of the outdoor environment.

TOURIST INFORMATION CENTRES

Oban	-	01631 563122
Tyndrum	-	01838 400246
Crieff	-	01764 652578
Perth	-	01738 638353
St. Andrews	-	01334 472021

USEFUL ADDRESSES

Long Distance Walkers Association
Brian Smith
10 Temple Park Close, Leeds LS15 0JJ
Tel: 0113 264 2205
This association is set up to further the interests of those who enjoy long distance walking. Members receive a journal three times each year which includes information on all aspects of long distance walking.

Ramblers Association
1-5 Wandsworth Road, London SW8 2XX
Advice and information on all walking matters. Local groups with regular meetings.

National Trust for Scotland
5 Charlotte Sq, Edinburgh EH2 4DU

Scottish Rights of Way Society Ltd.
Unit 2, John Cotton Business Centre
10/12 Sunnyside, Edinburgh EH7 5RA

Scottish Youth Hostels Association
7 Glebe Terrace, Stirling FK8 2JA

GLOSSARY OF WORDS

Bearing - *A degree or number of degrees set on a compass, follow the direction of travel arrow walking on that bearing to reach your intended destination.*

Burn - *Scottish word meaning stream, brook, beck or watercourse.*

Cairn - *An ancient stone mound erected as a marker. Often modern day piles of stones that denote a path or route are referred to as cairns.*

Col - *A pass or saddle between two hills. It provides access between one valley and another.*

Crag - *A steep rugged rock or peak.*

Escape Route - *Used for any emergency situation or in times of bad visibility. The main aim is to get you down to lower ground by the safest and quickest way.*

Glen - *Scottish word for a valley.*

Grid Reference - *Derived from the national grid reference system. This is used to pinpoint a place on a map by use of letters and numbers, written as G.R.- - - - - -*

Gully - *A narrow channel or cleft in a rock face, may have waterfalls, can be very slippery and have vertical drops.*

Kissing Gate - *Swing gate that usually lets one person through at a time by moving the gate backwards and forwards.*

Loch - *Scottish word for lake.*

Magnetic Bearing - *This is a grid bearing taken from a map and the relevant magnetic variation added to it to obtain the magnetic bearing. See the relevant maps for details of current magnetic variation.*

Metalled Road - *Generally known as a stone chipping road. This term evolved and became regarded as the roads metal or the roads surface.*

Outcrop - *Part of a rock formation that sticks out from the main body of rock.*

Plateau - *A wide and mainly flat area of elevated land.*

Route Card - *A plan of action prepared before you leave. A copy to be left with someone so that if you fail to return by a planned time then help can be summoned.*

Summit - *The highest point of a mountain or hill.*

Tarn - *A small mountain lake.*

Trig Point - *True name is Triangulation Pillar. These mark the summit of many mountains but not all. It is a small stone pillar with a number on it. The height of the mountain is taken from this point.*

NOTES

NOTES